Hell Within: Understanding Your Inner Demonland

Ali Ahmad

Published by Ali Ahmad, 2023.

HELL WITHIN: UNDERSTANDING YOUR INNER DEMONLAND

First edition. September 9, 2023.

ISBN: 979-8223317982

Written by Ali Ahmad.

Also by Ali Ahmad

Mental Cornucopia
Mental Cornucopia
The 24-Hour Productivity Hack
A.I and Ethical Writing
Hell Within: Understanding Your Inner Demonland

Table of Contents

Dedicated to the kurds.

Introduction: Personal Note

There are a lot of reasons behind writing this book. But the main one is that the mental world is becoming more dominated by external forces. Also, let us not forget how important this matter is. The mental world is all we have and all we live with. — When we sit alone, we are with our thoughts and our perceptions of the world, which might or might not be true at all.

But as we can see, this book is not just about your inner self. It is also about the demons within. The evil that is lurking around inside every one of us. — This book tries to address these demonic energies.

I have outlined some fundamental mental problems that each of us faces in this world. I know that this list is short and not enough. And God knows how many other mental problems and demonic energies are out there. But I think this book will be a great beginning for an open discussion on said matter.

I know this book is not religious, but we must never forget that many religious concepts are expressed through metaphors, and this book uses a lot of metaphorical language, especially the term <demon> In this book, demon is used to refer to negative thoughts or behaviors. We are primarily discussing thoughts because many of the behaviors in our modern era stem from thoughts rather than intentional actions. The term demon represents that thought which leads to doing bad things, such as murdering another human being, breaking other people's hearts, or neglecting to help the poor and the needy. All these problems arise from the demons within.

With my intensive thinking on this matter, I do believe that evilness cannot originate within a person's consciousness. It must come from another force that motivates this consciousness to do harm. Based on my experience and analysis, humans cannot create things; they can only assemble parts to create things. Take a car, for example, what is it made of? ... It is comprised of many parts. Now, can someone make this car without assembling the parts? ... We can see that this physical process follows a pattern. You cannot magically summon a car without assembling it. Therefore, evil thoughts also seem to have a similar nature to our own physical reality.

I hope that readers of this book find the materials useful and enjoyable, and any criticism that arises from this reading session is always welcomed and needed. I hope that readers realize the importance of the subject. All I want from this book is to bring awareness to the said matter.

Introduction: Book Summary

This book explores our inner world and how it is influenced by our thoughts and emotions. It talks about the <demons> within us, which are negative thoughts and behaviors. These demons can lead us to make bad choices and hurt ourselves and others. The book is not about actual demons but uses this word to describe harmful thoughts.

This book discusses various mental problems and patterns that many of us face. These problems include overthinking, procrastination, self-sabotage, and more. The book emphasizes the importance of recognizing and overcoming these patterns to lead a happier life.

It also talks about missed opportunities and time wasted on unimportant things. The author [Ali Ahmad] encourages readers to make the most of their time and not let regrets hold them back.

The book ends by discussing how to recognize and break free from negative patterns in our thinking and behavior. It encourages introspection and understanding the root causes of these patterns.

Overall, "Hell Within" aims to help readers become aware of their inner struggles and find ways to overcome them, leading to personal growth and a more fulfilling life.

Introduction: Book Terminology

Chapter 1

Inner Maze: The metaphorical representation of one's own thoughts and mental processes, often described as a complex labyrinth where one navigates through their thoughts and emotions.

Thought-Clothes: An allegorical reference to the idea that thoughts can be disguised or hidden beneath the surface, not always immediately apparent.

Demons: Symbolic of negative or harmful thoughts, emotions, or patterns of thinking that can hinder personal growth and well-being.

Reality Shaping: The concept that one's thoughts have the power to influence their perception of reality and can impact their life's outcomes and experiences.

Positive Thoughts: Thoughts that contribute to a sense of well-being, happiness, and personal growth.

Negative Thoughts: Thoughts that are detrimental to one's mental and emotional state, potentially leading to negative emotions and behaviors.

Conflicting Thoughts: The state where opposing or contradictory thoughts or ideas exist simultaneously within a person's mind, often causing inner turmoil.

Establish Order: The act of taking control of one's thoughts, analyzing conflicting ideas, and deciding which thoughts align with their goals and values.

Inner Kingdom: A metaphorical term for one's inner world or mental landscape, which can be organized and harmonious when thoughts are aligned with one's purpose.

Inner Critic: The inner voice that criticizes and judges one's actions and decisions, often negatively affecting self-esteem and confidence.

Self-Esteem: The value and confidence one has in themselves and their abilities.

Overthinking: The act of excessively dwelling on thoughts and ideas, often leading to anxiety, stress, and a lack of focus on important matters.

Thought Loops: Repetitive patterns of thinking where the same thoughts or ideas continuously resurface without resolution.

Personal Growth: The process of self-improvement and development in various aspects of one's life.

Determination: The quality of being firm and resolute in pursuing one's goals.

Inner Demons: Negative thoughts and emotions that can consume one's mental and emotional well-being if not addressed or controlled.

Emotional Regulation: The ability to manage and control one's emotions.

Clarity: The state of having a clear and focused mind, free from confusion or doubt.

Purpose: A sense of direction or meaning in life, often motivating one to pursue specific goals and values.

Self-Improvement: The process of enhancing one's skills, knowledge, and personal qualities to become a better version of oneself.

Anxiety: A state of uneasiness or apprehension often caused by excessive worrying or overthinking.

Chapter 2

Addiction to Comfort: The tendency to prioritize comfort and familiarity over pursuing dreams and challenges.

Comfort Zones: A state of familiarity and safety where individuals avoid taking risks or facing challenges.

Potential: The capabilities and possibilities that individuals possess but may not realize when staying within their comfort zones.

Discipline: The ability to maintain self-control and resist the allure of immediate comfort in favor of long-term goals.

Challenge: A task or goal that requires effort, determination, and stepping outside of one's comfort zone.

Dreams: Aspirations, goals, or ambitions that individuals desire to achieve, often requiring them to break free from their comfort zones.

Settle: To accept mediocrity or less-than-ideal outcomes due to the comfort of the familiar.

Procrastination: The act of delaying tasks or activities, often due to fear, anxiety, or avoidance of feelings of inadequacy.

Laziness: A lack of motivation or effort to complete tasks or achieve goals.

Pressure: The stress and urgency associated with deadlines or expectations that can lead to procrastination.

Last-Minute Rush: The habit of completing tasks just before their deadline, often resulting in stress and exhaustion.

Motivation: The driving force or reason behind one's actions and efforts.

Time Management: The effective allocation and organization of one's time to achieve tasks and goals.

Stress Reduction: Techniques and strategies to alleviate stress and anxiety related to procrastination.

Satisfaction: The feeling of accomplishment and fulfillment that comes from completing tasks and achieving goals.

Passivity: A state of inactivity or lack of active engagement in tasks and goals.

Self-Sabotage: Deliberate or unconscious actions and behaviors that undermine one's own goals, well-being, or success.

Sabotage: The act of deliberately damaging or interfering with one's own progress, often due to deep-seated beliefs, fears, or past experiences.

Procrastination: A form of self-sabotage characterized by delaying tasks and activities.

Self-Doubt: Lack of confidence in one's abilities, which can lead to self-sabotaging behaviors.

Perfectionism: The pursuit of flawlessness or excessively high standards, which can hinder progress and lead to self-sabotage.

Comparisons: The act of measuring one's own abilities, achievements, or progress against others, potentially leading to self-doubt and self-sabotage.

Fear: Negative emotions, often irrational, that can hinder progress and lead to self-sabotaging behaviors.

Decisions: Choices and actions individuals make to either support their goals or contribute to self-sabotage.

Limitations: Self-imposed boundaries or beliefs that restrict personal growth and success.

Regrets: Feelings of disappointment or remorse related to past actions, which can contribute to self-sabotage.

Determination: The quality of being firm and resolute in pursuing one's goals, which can counteract self-sabotage.

Road to the Future: The path toward achieving future goals and aspirations, free from the hindrance of past regrets and self-sabotage.

Chapter 3

Missed Opportunities: Moments when individuals fail to seize chances or make choices that could have led to positive outcomes.

Regret: A feeling of sadness or disappointment over past actions or decisions.

Investment: Allocating resources or effort into a potential opportunity, often with the hope of gaining future benefits.

Innovative Startup: A newly established company or business that introduces new and creative ideas or technologies.

Stock Price: The current value of shares in a publicly traded company.

Hesitation: Pausing or delaying action due to uncertainty or doubt.

Fear of Change: The discomfort or reluctance to embrace new or unfamiliar situations.

Comfort Zone: A state of familiarity and safety where individuals avoid taking risks.

Overthinking: Excessively analyzing and considering various aspects of a situation or decision, often leading to inaction.

Catalyst for Change: A motivating factor or event that inspires individuals to make positive adjustments in their lives.

Time: The finite resource of moments that make up one's life.

Currency of Life: A metaphorical concept highlighting the value of time in shaping one's experiences and destiny.

Regret: A feeling of disappointment or remorse related to the misuse or waste of time.

Social Media: Online platforms and networks where individuals share and interact with content, often consuming time.

Scrolling: The act of browsing through content on social media feeds.

Digital Hell-fire: An allegorical reference to the excessive use of technology and social media that can lead to wasted time.

Procrastination: The act of delaying or postponing tasks or activities.

Priorities: The things or activities considered most important or valuable in one's life.

Binge-watching: Watching multiple episodes of a TV series in succession, often for an extended period.

Entertainment: Activities or content that provide enjoyment or amusement.

Habit: A regular and often unconscious behavior or practice.

Toxic Relationships: Relationships characterized by negativity, harm, or emotional drain.

Emotional Energy: The emotional and psychological resources individuals invest in relationships and interactions.

Positive Connections: Relationships and interactions that bring positivity, support, and enrichment to one's life.

Symphony of Life: A metaphorical representation of the entirety of one's life experiences and moments.

Meaningful Moments: Experiences and activities that hold personal significance and value in one's life journey.

Chapter 4

Mental Pain: Emotional distress or suffering experienced in the mind.

Inner Voice: The inner dialogue or thoughts that occur within a person's mind.

Demonic Energies: Metaphorical representation of negative and destructive thought patterns or emotions.

Inner Peace: A state of mental and emotional calm and contentment.

Proxy Attacks: Allegorical reference to moments when negative thoughts or emotions affect an individual's mental well-being.

Disobey: Failing to prioritize one's mental well-being or engage in actions contrary to one's best interests.

Good Deeds: Positive and morally upright actions or behaviors.

Overall Well-being: The state of being mentally, emotionally, and physically healthy and content.

Humanity: The collective group of human beings.

Inner Demons: Metaphorical representation of internal psychological or emotional obstacles that hinder personal growth and conflict resolution.

Conflict Resolution: The process of addressing and resolving disputes or disagreements between individuals or groups.

Fear of Change: The reluctance or discomfort associated with altering familiar routines or behaviors.

Ego: The sense of self or identity, which can include feelings of pride and self-importance.

Short-term Gratification: Seeking immediate satisfaction or pleasure.

Vulnerability: The state of being open to emotional or psychological harm.

Emotional Openness: The willingness to express and share one's feelings and emotions.

Drama: Situations or interactions characterized by excessive emotion, conflict, or excitement.

Self-sabotage: Engaging in behaviors or thoughts that undermine personal goals or well-being.

Self-doubt: A lack of confidence or belief in one's abilities.

Negative Self-image: A pessimistic or critical perception of oneself.

Inner Landscapes: Metaphorical representation of one's inner thoughts, emotions, and psychological experiences.

Repetitive Patterns: Recurring behaviors, thoughts, or emotions that persist over time.

Psyche: The innermost aspects of one's mind, including thoughts, emotions, and consciousness.

Cure: A solution or remedy to address and alleviate negative patterns.

Introspection: The act of examining and reflecting on one's thoughts, emotions, and experiences.

Triggers: Events or stimuli that elicit specific emotional or behavioral responses.

Footprints: Metaphorical signs or indications of a recurring pattern.

Past Traumas: Negative or distressing experiences from one's history that can impact current thoughts and behaviors.

Dig Deep: Engaging in self-exploration or seeking the root causes of patterns.

Trusted Friend: A person in whom one has confidence and can confide.

Therapist: A trained mental health professional who provides counseling and support.

Break Free: To escape the influence or control of a negative pattern.

Chapter 1 — Inner Maze

Chapter 1 — Inner Maze

1.1 Your Thoughts

In this section, we are dealing with demons covered in thought-clothes trying to come off as an ordinary simple thought ...

Remember, this is a maze, a never-ending game ...

In this maze you are with your own thoughts. — Understand this: your thoughts are not passing ideas; they shape your reality. They can influence how you see the world, the choices you make, and who you become. Thoughts are everything.

Every day, your mind is filled with all sorts of thoughts, from everyday stuff to deep thinking. Some thoughts may seem unimportant, while others can change your life.

Do not overlook how powerful your thoughts are. They have a big impact on your daily life, your goals, and the path your life takes. They can shape your reality. And they are shaping the reality that we are in, daily.

Your thoughts are a maze in which you spend most of your time. You navigate through it, seeking exit doors and discovering inner pathways to other ideas and mental games.

In this maze you have the power to make your thoughts become real. When you truly think about something and work toward it, you begin to make it happen. It is not just hoping; it is like giving a strong order to the universe. Take control of your thoughts, for they determine what your future will be like. Use this power wisely, and you will see your thoughts change your life.

Thoughts can change emotions. Your thoughts affect how you feel. Happy thoughts can make you feel good, while sad thoughts can make you feel bad.

So, It is important to be aware of what you are thinking. Try to think positive and hopeful thoughts, and it will make you feel happier inside. This happiness will also show in how you interact with others and how your relationships go. Think of your thoughts as colours on a canvas, so choose the bright and cheerful ones to paint a happier picture for yourself. — If you feed negative thoughts, the demons, they will grown. So be careful what and which thought are you entertaining.

Contemplating on negative ideas equals negative results. In this maze, you are the main character. Do not feed the demons inside.

"A thought, even a possibility, can shatter and transform us."

— Friedrich Wilhelm Nietzsche

Chapter 1 — Inner Maze

1.2 Conflicting Thoughts

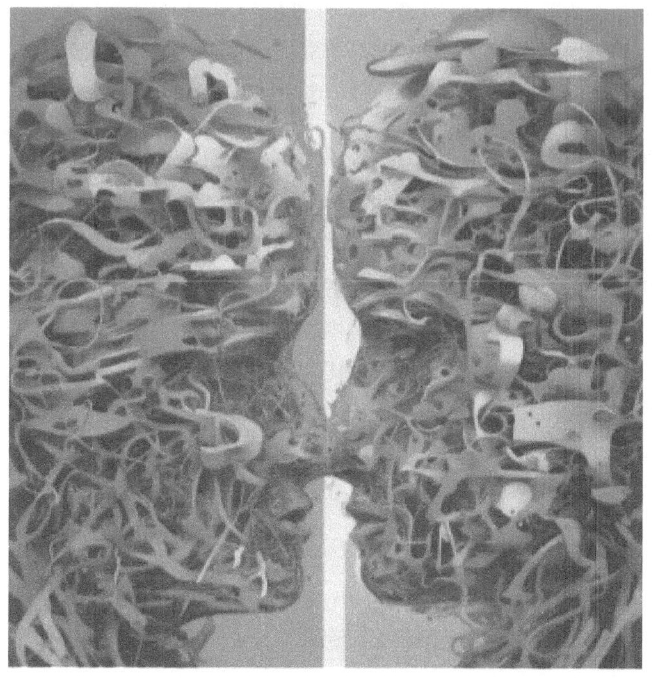

In the demonland of your mind, conflicts between thoughts are a battleground where you must **<<<Establish Order>>>**.

When opposing ideas clash within you, take charge. Analyze and rank them. Decide which ones serve your goals and values best. Cast aside the thoughts that hinder your progress like dead-weight.

Command your mind to align with your true purpose. Command your mind to align with you.

Do not allow contradictory thoughts create chaos ... Put your authority over your mental landscape ... When doubt and uncertainty creep in, confront them head-on. Demand clarity and certainty from your thoughts. Insist on a clear path forward and delete confusion from your <**Inner Kingdom**>.

Your thoughts are soldiers in the battle for your mental clarity. Train them to obey your command. Discipline your mind like a general leading an army. Rally your thoughts behind your chosen direction and dismiss those that resist. Your inner world is a reflection of your outer reality, so ensure it is an organized and harmonious reality. — When your thoughts become demons [and they are demons ...] you should be careful about deciding which thoughts worth the thinking effort or not. It is crazy how much energy people waste on thinking about demonic thoughts ...

Based on that, conflicting thoughts can be like turbulent storms in your inner world. But you are the captain of this ship, and it is time to steer it in the right direction. When you control your thoughts you will realize how important it is to actually command your own mental landscape.

When you sense the conflicting thoughts, take control of them. Steer towards the thoughts that steer you towards your goals, and cut through the storm of uncertainty with <**determination**>.

Remember, in the Inner Maze, conflicting thoughts are but challenges to overcome. Rise above them with the unwavering command of your will. Embrace the power to choose which thoughts rule your mind. Let your decisions be a declaration of your intent, and may your thoughts march in towards the path you have chosen. You are the master of your inner domain, and harmony awaits those who lead with purpose. — Your inner kingdom.

"Every now and then a man's mind is stretched by a new idea or sensation, and never shrinks back to its former dimensions."

— Oliver Wendell Holmes Sr., Autocrat of the Breakfast Table

Chapter 1 — Inner Maze

1.3 The Inner Critic

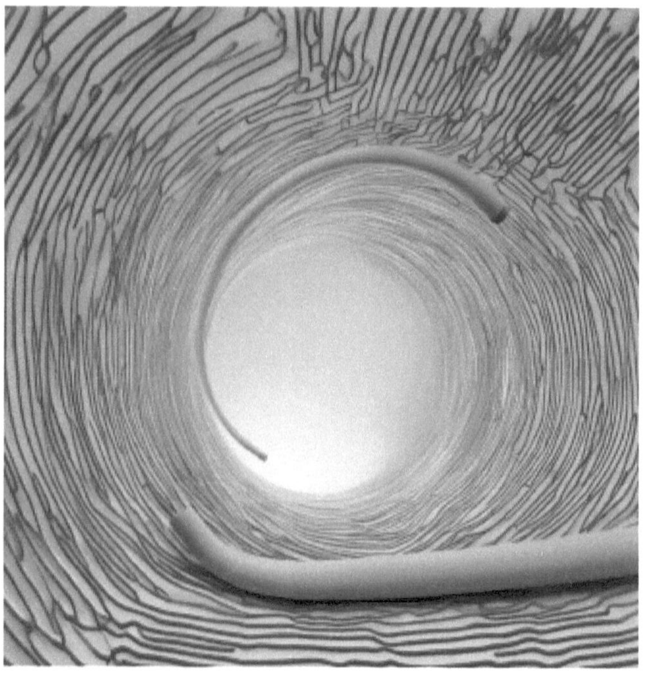

Listen closely, for it is time to deal with a persistent presence inside you: **the Inner Critic**. This inner voice, hidden deep within [the demonland], often acts like a strict judge. It carefully looks at what you do, every choice you make, every mistake you have, and criticizes them harshly.

But here is the main point: you need to take control of the Inner Critic because it only holds you back and hurts your self-esteem. It pretends to protect you but actually works against you, and it is time to stop it.

When the Inner Critic shows up, do not back down. Instead, stand strong and determined because you are in charge. Tell it to stop its constant negative comments. Ask it to focus on giving helpful advice instead of criticism.

Your inner thoughts should help and motivate you, not make you feel bad. Make the Inner Critic your friend, not your enemy. Tell it to give you advice that helps you grow and get better, instead of dragging you down. — Train your Critic to work with you and for you. Do not train it to go against you and your goals/ideals ...

Remember, you control your thoughts, and the Inner Critic is just a part of your inner world. You have the power to change how it acts. Use your authority to turn it into something that helps and improves you.

The Inner Critic becomes stronger when you pay too much attention to it. So, focus on being kind to yourself and believing in yourself. Tell your inner voice to motivate and guide you toward your goals and dreams. It is time to take control of your inner world and stop the Inner Critic from being so negative. You can do it. By moving your focus on another thought. There are a lot of thoughts in your inner world. Focus on the most important ones only.

Now is the time to lead with confidence and kindness, creating a mental space that encourages growth, strength, and self-improvement. The demons hate these kind of words. So it is important to use them the most.

"In the inner courtroom of my mind, mine is the only judgment that counts."

— Nathaniel Branden, Six Pillars of Self-Esteem

Chapter 1 — Inner Maze

1.4 Overthinking

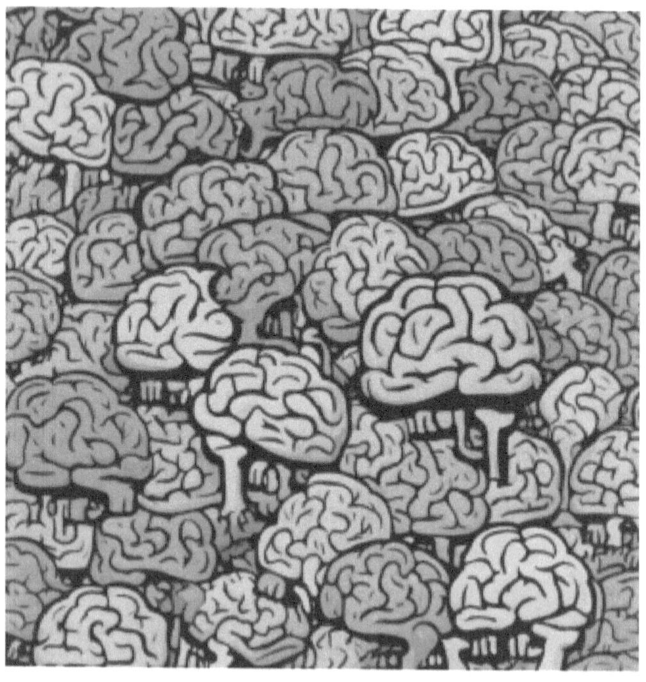

The demonland wants you to overthink because when you overthink, you lose sight of what is important. And you will tremble down to your lowest levels of energies. — Overthinking is another weapon that demons use to stop you from growing.

Overthinking is when your brain goes into overdrive, like a car engine revving too fast. It is when you think about something so much that it feels like your brain is running in circles, an endless cycle of nothingness.

Imagine this: you have a puzzle in front of you, and you want to solve it. Overthinking is when you keep trying to put the same puzzle piece in the same spot, even though it clearly does not fit. You keep doing it over and over, hoping it will magically work. But it will not.

Overthinking can happen to anyone, kids, grown-ups, and everyone in between. It is like having too many tabs open on a computer — your brain gets all jumbled up with thoughts, and it can be hard to focus on one thing.

Sometimes, overthinking can make you worry about things that have not even happened yet. It is like imagining a monster under your bed when there is nothing there. Your brain can create problems that do not exist, and it can make you feel anxious or stressed without any possible reasons.

But here is the thing: you can tell your brain to slow down. You can say, "Hey brain, let us take a break." It is like hitting pause on a movie when you need a break. You can take a deep breath, go for a walk, or talk to someone you trust. Sometimes it is best to just leave it alone and go somewhere else. Sometimes the demons/thoughts are too strong to handle ... we [humans] are weak, therefore it is important to just go out or ask for outside help instead of "inside help".

But when you stop overthinking, it is like clearing away the clouds in your mind, and you can see things more clearly. You can focus on what is important and not get stuck in a loop of thoughts — thought loops.

So, remember, overthinking is like a puzzle piece that does not fit. Take a break, clear your mind, and you will find that the pieces start falling into place. It is something we all deal with, but with a little practice, you can tame that overthinking monster in your mind.

"To think too much is a disease."

— Fyodor Dostoyevsky, Notes from Underground & The Double

Chapter 2 — Reality Escaped

Chapter 2 — Reality Escaped

2.1 Addiction to Comfort

It is not just about comfort; it is about doing what is necessary and right in this moment ...

We have to discuss something that can really hold us back — being too comfortable all the time. It is like getting stuck in a cozy but confining bubble that stops us from going after our dreams. It has been known for centuries that in the demonland pleasure and comfort is highly regarded and placed on a pedestal

This addiction to comfort tricks us into remaining in our comfort zones, where everything feels safe and easy. But guess what? ... — That is where our potential gets buried. To break free, we need to see comfort as the sneaky enemy it is and fight back with everything we have. It is really hard to fight pleasure without discipline. Therefore, we must stay strong.

Comfort makes us hold on to the same old stuff, the things we know well. We like it there because there are not many challenges or risks. But that is exactly why our dreams and good deeds do not come true. To chase those dreams, we have to break out of that hell-land and tackle challenges head-on.

The grip of comfort is not just about where we are physically — it interferes with our thoughts and feelings too. It tricks us into choosing what is easy and quick over what is tough but rewarding. This addiction turns us into people who settle for "just okay" instead of going after our big dreams and deeds.

"Every form of addiction is bad, no matter whether the narcotic be alcohol, morphine or idealism."

— Carl Gustav Jung

Chapter 2 — Reality Escaped

2.2 Procrastination

Understanding and Overcoming Procrastination in Demonland:

In the realm of Demonland, many folks battle an enemy called procrastination. It is not just laziness; people here often work hard but with fear and anxiety. — We need to understand why this happens and how to escape it.

Some in Demonland blame laziness, while others believe they do better under pressure. But most have not tried working systematically, so they can not be sure. — Some even say they enjoy last-minute rushes, but they forget the stress and exhaustion it brings.

Procrastination is not just poor time management. It runs deeper and is worse in places like schools, where constant evaluations happen. Procrastination can be a way to protect yourself. It is an excuse to avoid feeling inadequate. When there is pressure to do well, humans often procrastinate due to fear and anxiety — fear of failure, success, looking foolish ...

So, how can you escape this cycle?

We will use the <**RMRA**> model here:

R = step 1: Recognize

M = step 2: Manage

R = step 3: Reasons

A = step 4: Active

Demonstration:

Step 1: Recognize the Problem

To escape procrastination, first, understand why it happens and how it helps you when you quit it. — Knowing this can help you resist it.

For example: I have work to do but instead, I am wasting time on having fun. Now, I have recognized the problem. This is the first step.

Step 2: Manage Your Time

Good time management is essential for deleting any negative activities. After selecting your problem, you can manage it in a perfectly harmonious timeline.

Warning: always remember that <time management> is not enough. Avoid techniques that make you more anxious. Choose ones that reduce stress and focus on the satisfaction of finishing tasks.

Step 3: Find Good Reasons

To beat procrastination, stay motivated for the right reasons. Fear-driven motivations, like fear of failing or trying to outdo others, do not work well. Instead, focus on goals that make you feel good and help you learn. You must have a good reason for your goals.

Step 4: Stay Active

Being passive is a problem. Engage actively in what you are doing, seek out what interests you, set goals, and do not be afraid to ask questions. And you must always learn.

"You may delay, but time will not."

— Benjamin Franklin

Chapter 2 — Reality Escaped

2.3 Self-Sabotage

The term <sabotage> is a verb that means to deliberately damage, destroy, or interfere with equipment, weapons, buildings, or plans in order to hinder the success of an enemy, competitor, or a particular action. [Online Cambridge Dictionary 2023]

<Self-sabotage> refers to the deliberate or unconscious actions and behaviors that individuals engage in, which undermine their own goals, well-being, or success. It involves behaviors or thought patterns that work against one's best interests, often stemming from deep-seated beliefs, fears, or past experiences.

Self-sabotage can manifest in various forms, such as procrastination, self-doubt, perfectionism, negative self-talk, or engaging in harmful habits ...

Alright, let us break this down in a simpler way:

Stop Self-Sabotage: You are your own worst enemy, smashing your dreams to bits. It is time to stop and become your own success architect.

Procrastination Sucks: Imagine a black hole in your brain gobbling up motivation. That is procrastination. Flip the switch, start now, not tomorrow.

Excuse Factory: Stop being the gold medalist in making excuses like "I am too tired" or "It is too hard." Embrace truth, watch self-sabotage crumble. It is hard to be truthful but, it is the truth. And in the end, it is the truth that ultimately matter the most.

Delete Perfectionism: Spending ages on perfection is just <fancy procrastination>. It is just a fancy way of being a professional procrastinator. Instead, Aim for excellence, not perfection. Imperfections most of the time breed creativity. So it is very crucial to make mistakes and keep on going.

Kill Self-Doubt: Confidence is your safety net. Believe in yourself; you are more capable than you think. Of course if you put your potential into practice. That way, it will be more beautiful.

No More Comparisons: Comparing yourself to others is like comparing apples, oranges, and pineapples. Focus on your unique journey, not theirs. And maybe you are even more important than them and you do not even know it. Because comparisons kill potentials.

Face Your Fears: Fear is a spooky carnival ride. Escape its maze; fear is just a shadow with no substance. Fear can be helpful in certain situations, but right now, in this epoch, most of what we fear drives us to failure.

Choose Decisions: Sometimes, a wrong decision is better than none. But always choose the best decisions in life. And choose.

Shatter Limitations: there is a glass ceiling above you. Can you see it? ... Break it. — Do not limit yourself with <**self-made boundaries**>; reach new heights.

Road to the Future: Do not drive forward while staring in the rear-view mirror of past regrets. Focus on the road ahead. Learn from mistakes and move forward with determination into your potential future. Always

"Resistance by definition is self-sabotage."

— Steven Pressfield (The War of Art: Winning the Inner Creative Battle)

Chapter 3 — Regrets

3.1 Missed Opportunities

3.2 Time-wasters

Chapter 3 — Regrets

3.1 Missed Opportunities

Missed opportunities‹ are similar to stars in the night sky. They twinkle with promise, but if you do not reach for them, they remain distant and unattainable. It is time to address the regret of opportunities left unseized, those moments when you hesitated, and the door of potential slowly closed.

Imagine a time when you had a chance to invest in that innovative startup, but you let doubt amd fear creep in. The stock price skyrocketed, and you were left watching from the sidelines. Those moments are like sand slipping through your fingers — they cannot be recaptured. Regret can sting like a swarm of bees, but it is not too late to change the inner narrative.

Opportunities often come disguised as challenges. That job offer in another city that you turned down because you feared change — that could have been the leap your career needed. The fear of the unknown held you back, but life's greatest rewards often lie on the other side of comfort.

Sometimes, missed opportunities are a result of overthinking. You analyze every angle, every potential failures, until the opportunity goes away. Inaction becomes your default mode, and you are left with a sinking feeling in your gut, wondering what could have been.

The regret of missed opportunities is a bitter pill to swallow, but it can also be a catalyst for change. Use it as fuel for future activities. Let those moments of hesitation teach you to grab the next chance that comes your way. Learn from the past, but do not let it change your future.

Remember, regret can be a powerful teacher. It is a reminder that life is full of chances waiting to be taken. So, the next time an opportunity knocks, answer with boldness and enthusiasm. Embrace the unknown, for it is where growth and transformation come.

"men of experience say, "Four things do not come back: the spoken word, the sped arrow, the past life, and the neglected opportunity."

— Ted Chiang, Exhalation

Chapter 3 — Regrets

3.2 Time-wasters

Time is the currency of life, time is the real money, and how you spend it shapes your destiny. Yet, in the grand landscape of time, there are moments when you look back and cringe at the hours, days, or even years wasted on the doings that added little to no value to your life.

Consider the hours spent scrolling through social media feeds, mindlessly liking and sharing content that barely leaves a trace [of importance]. It is like tossing your precious time into a digital hell-fire, where moments slip away like grains of sand through an hourglass. The regret of those wasted hours can be a bitter pill and destroy you in the future. Especially when you remember the wasted times and the wasted potentials ...

Or think about the countless hours spent [binge-]watching TV series that, in the end, leave you with nothing but fading memories of fictional worlds ... You are living in fiction. — Do not get me wrong; entertainment has its place, but when it becomes a habit that consumes your days, it is time to re-evaluate your priorities.

Procrastination, too, is a notorious time-waster. You delay important tasks, convincing yourself that you will get to them eventually. But "eventually" often turns into "never," and you are left with unfinished projects and nagging regret.

Let us not forget about toxic relationships that drain your time and emotional energy. Those friendships or partnerships that bring more negativity than positivity into your life are not worth the investment. Regretting the time spent on such relationships is a reminder to surround yourself with those who uplift you and support you.

In the grand symphony of life, every moment counts. So, let the regret of wasted time serve as a reminder to make the most of each day. Redirect your focus towards the activities that enrich your life, nurture your positive passions, and strengthen your positive connections. The clock is ticking, and it is never too late to compose a masterpiece of meaningful moments.

"When you kill time, remember that it has no resurrection."

— A.W. Tozer

Chapter 4 — Pattern Recognition

4.1 Mental Pain

There can be a lot of classes and identifications of mental pains. But some mental pains are actually more demonic rather than a sickness to the mental.

When you are mentally feeling pain, about someone or about financial matters, always remember that this inner voice is just with itself for its own interests and deep negative rooted beliefs. Remember that this pain does not and will not and will never care about you. It is there to hunt you down and make you its own puppet slave.

Of course, there are real mental pains, such as mental disorders like schizophrenia and related illusionary disorders. — But what we are dealing with here is that most of our mental pains and thoughts are not actually sickness but legit demons attacking your inner peace and forcing you to do things that you will never want to be done upon you. But you do it anyway because you trust the inner demons.

A mental pain about missing someone or wishing to be with someone, or gaining money, is a total attack upon your consciousness. This symptom is a sign that the demonic energies are surrounding you, and you must stand your ground and shield yourself as soon as possible. Before these demons win the battle against you, which sometimes they can if you put yourself lower than them.

In a day, you can see there are a lot of these [Proxy] attacks that can mentally crush you down and drain you. Understand this: Anytime you disobey your highest mental well-being and goodness, you lay the path open for the evils to crawl inside your inner tomb. — These mental attacks can be frequent in a day, or they can be none. — They can change from day to day living, but always remember that every single individual on this earth has the same mental battle-ground experience as you. So always be kind and forgive the things that are small in scale and the things that do not really matter to the overall well-being of humanity and good deeds of the universe.

"Mental suffering is an inferno started, and kept burning, by thinking; and its smoke sometimes leaves one crying."

— Mokokoma Mokhonoana

Chapter 4 — Pattern Recognition

4.2 Resolve Conflicts

One way our inner demons resist conflict resolution is by instilling a fear of change. Conflict resolution often requires us to step out of our comfort zones, adapt to new situations, and alter our behaviors. Our inner demons thrive on familiarity and resist change at all costs, making it challenging to embrace conflict resolution as a means of personal growth.

Our inner demons are closely tied to our big egos. When conflicts arise, our big egos can be bruised as we confront our mistakes, flaws, or the need to compromise. The inner demon will do everything it can to protect our big negative ego, even if it means avoiding conflict resolution altogether. It feeds on our insecurities and the desire to maintain a positive self-image.

Inner demons prioritize short-term gratification over long-term benefits. Resolving conflicts often requires patience and delayed rewards ... Inner demons crave immediate satisfaction and can persuade us to give in to our impulses, resulting in the perpetuation of conflicts rather than their resolution.

Conflict resolution often demands vulnerability, honesty, and emotional openness. Our inner demons despise vulnerability because it makes us feel exposed and uncomfortable. They convince us that avoiding conflict is the safer option, even if it ultimately destroy our personal growth and relationships.

Also about dramas: Inner demons thrive on drama and chaos. They enjoy seeing conflicts escalate because it provides them with a sense of excitement and significance. This can lead to a subconscious desire to perpetuate conflicts rather than resolve them, as they fuel the inner demon's need for excitement and attention.

The most insidious way our inner demons hinder conflict resolution is through self-sabotage. They whisper self-doubt and negativity in our ears, making us believe we are incapable of resolving conflicts successfully. This self-sabotage can manifest as procrastination, avoidance, or even aggressive behavior that exacerbates conflicts.

This inner voice demands you to lift up your big ego even more than it has been lifted and enlarge it forever more ... And never lower yourself down to resolve conflicts. The inner demon within whispers: "oh how you let yourself be this weak!? ... Do not weaken yourself! ... Let them fight! ... If you resolve they will think you are weak! ..."

"Human happiness is defined by the hardships and conflicts you have been through. The greater they are, the greater is your happiness."

— Peter Deunov

4.3 Recognizing a Pattern

Our inner landscapes, often concealed in the depths of our psyche, can be running with repetitive and repeating patterns that can manifest as inner demons. These patterns, similar to ruts in a well-worn road, can keep us trapped in a cycle of negative emotions, thoughts, and behaviors. Recognizing and understanding these demonic patterns is the crucial first step towards finding a cure and putting an end to their relentless recurrence.

To begin with, it is essential to acknowledge that our inner demons are not entirely mystical or impossible to hunt down.

Instead, they are the result of our experiences, thoughts, and emotions weaving a web of habits and reactions over time. This web, like a spider's intricate design, may appear daunting at first, but it is not that scary in actuality.

One way to unearth these patterns is through >**introspection**<, a simple act of looking within ourselves with curiosity and honesty. This does not require a PhD in psychology but a willingness to explore our thoughts and emotions with an open heart. Pay attention to recurring thoughts, emotions, or behaviors that make you feel trapped or unhappy. Do you often find yourself reacting to certain situations in a similar way? ... Are there particular triggers that consistently set off a negative chain of events? ... Identifying these patterns is like finding footprints left by a persistent creature in the forest of your mind. And there are always patterns to problems. Which can make it easier for us to solve these problems.

Once identified, the next step is to analyze the origin of these patterns. Demonic patterns are like vines that creep into our consciousness, often taking root in past traumas or negative experiences. It is much needed to dig deep, sometimes with the help of a trusted friend or an honest therapist, to unearth the underlying causes. Understanding why these patterns exist can shed light on how to break free from their grip.

Let us analyze a problem that contains a pattern:

[1] I hit my cat.

[2] My cat screams.

[3] I hate screaming; therefore, I cry.

The main problem in this situation for me:

I hate it when cats scream.

But in actuality, there was a clear pattern. It is not that you hate cats screaming; it is that you are making this happen daily. And the failure to recognize the pattern leads you to repeating it. And thus making you even more miserable.

"I am not that air, I am the pattern that it assumed, temporarily."

— Ted Chiang, Exhalation

Appendix

Related Books

Bonus Art

Related Books

here are some books the readers will benefit from:

Daniel Kahneman - Thinking, Fast and Slow, 2013.

Simon Blackburn - Think: A Compelling Introduction to Philosophy, 1999.

Tim Hurson - Think Better: An Innovator's Guide to Productive Thinking, 2010.

Chase Hill, Scott Sharp - How to Stop Overthinking: The 7-Step Plan to Control and Eliminate Negative Thoughts, Declutter Your Mind and Start Thinking Positively in 5 Minutes or Less, 2019

Marvin Bergfeld - Negative People, Negative Thoughts: Dealing With Negative People, Negative Thinking, Criticism and Envy. Overcome Negative Feelings and Negativity, 2019

Religious Texts:

The Quran

The Bible

Bonus Art

Bonus art by the book cover designer

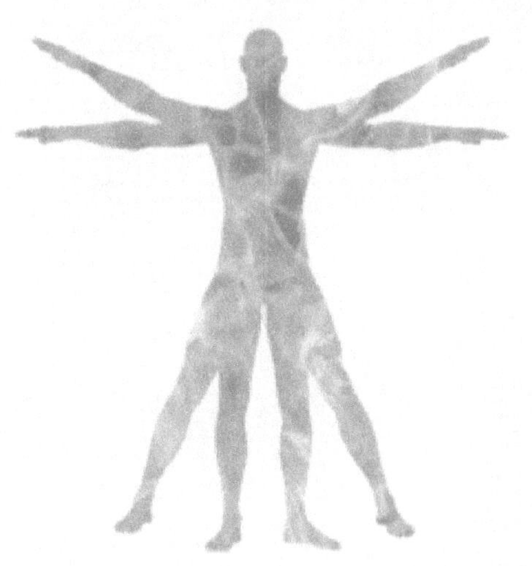

(@fuji_xv)

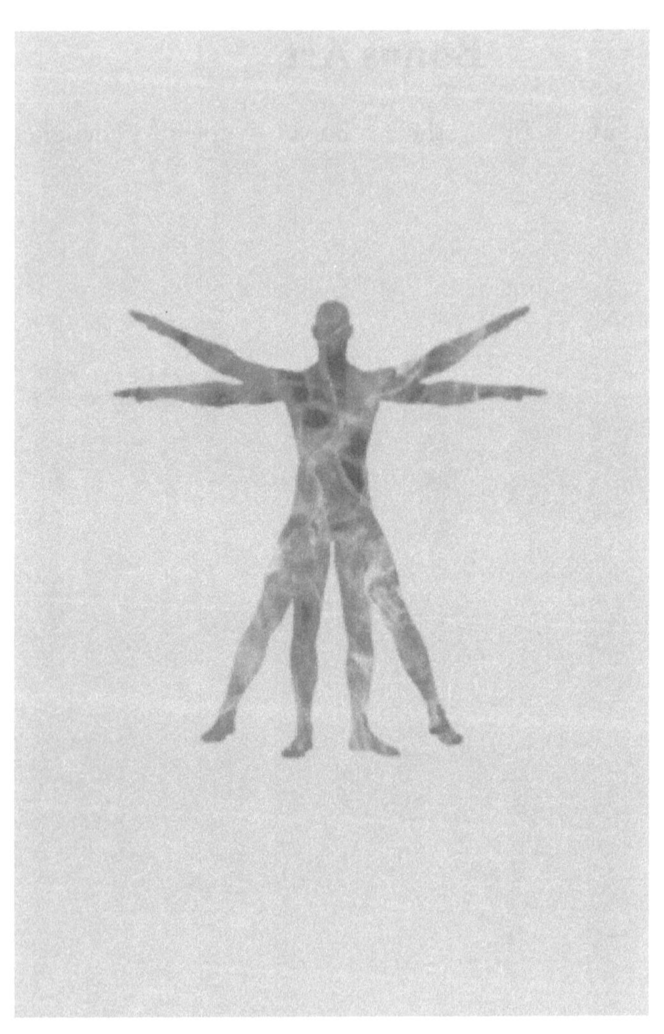

HELL
WITHIN
Understanding Your Inner
Demonland
ALI AHMAD

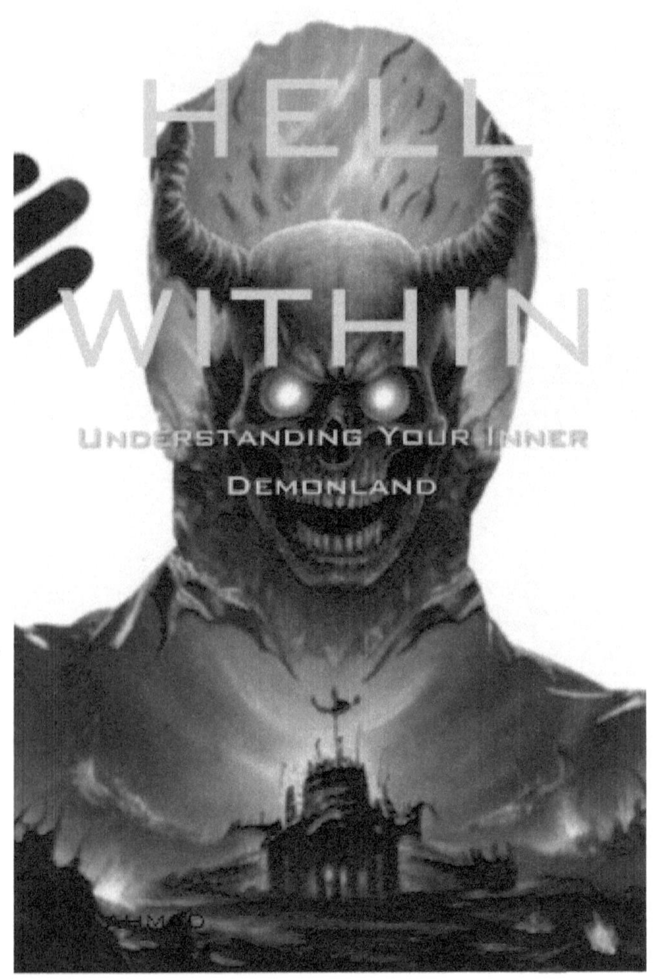

HELL
WITHIN
Understanding Your Inner
Demonland

HELL
WITHIN
Understanding Your Inner
Demonland

HELL
WITHIN
UNDERSTANDING YOUR INNER
DEMONLAND
ALI AHMAD

Don't miss out!

Visit the website below and you can sign up to receive emails whenever Ali Ahmad publishes a new book. There's no charge and no obligation.

https://books2read.com/r/B-A-DDUZ-OVWNC

BOOKS 2 READ

Connecting independent readers to independent writers.

Also by Ali Ahmad

Mental Cornucopia
Mental Cornucopia
The 24-Hour Productivity Hack
A.I and Ethical Writing
Hell Within: Understanding Your Inner Demonland

About the Author

Ali Ahmad

I am a Kurdish writer who strives to produce better content and information for the overall benefit of humanity, and to bring knowledge to others around the globe.

Contacts

Mail: ali.ahmad.krd@gmail

Youtube: Ali.Ahmad.H

Instagram: ali.ahmad.krd

Tiktok : ali.ahmad.h

Release Designer

Instagram : Fuji_xv

Whatsapp : +9647512308044

Works

<u>kurdish</u>

مرۆڤ لە لووتکەدا؛ هەولێک بۆ باشترکردنی ژیان

چۆن قسه بکەین

ئەخلاق بە سادەیی

وەهمی سەرکەوتن

چەند سەرنجێک لەسەر ڕووخساریەت: ژیل دۆلۆز و فیلێکس گواتاری

چەند سەرنجێک لەسەر تەمەن

ئاشنابوون بە زانستی ژیربێژی

هەشت یاسای جەنگەڵ

<u>English</u>

9. Mental Cornucopia

10. The 24-Hour Productivity Hack

11. A.I and Ethical Writing

12. Hell Within: Understanding Your Inner Demonland